FROM SIN & SHAME TO GLORY

Biblical Principles and Facts of Addiction Recovery

Authored by Pastor Carl Flowers

Trinity Outreach Publishing
502 Jarrell St
Picayune, MS 39466

For information address Trinity Outreach Publishing Rights Department, 502 Jarrell St, Picayune, MS 39466

First Paperback edition August 2016

Manufactured in the United States of America

ISBN-13: 978-0692770078

ISBN-10: 0692770070

It is my prayer that this will be made available to Christian bookstores and distributors worldwide.

DEDICATION

To the most caring and wonderful woman in the world, my precious wife, Julie for her increasing Love and commitment to me, our Family, and the kingdom of God.

To my son, Justin, to my Daughter Tayla, to my grandchildren, Ra'Nyra, Jaidyn, and Nova Flowers.

To my church family and staff at Trinity Outreach Ministries, who faithfully loved and supported me over the years.

To my Mother Joyce I Mclaurin, who has faithfully labored, physically and prayerfully on my behalf.

To my Spiritual Father, Apostle Jimmy Peters and to all the leaders and Coaches who invested in my life.

To all the men and women who looked to me as a father & mentor; because of you, this book has come to fruition.

To my Lord and Savior, who has delivered and set me free, who has made all things possible for me.

FORWARD

I had the opportunity to be a school counselor in the Avondale School District for thirty-six years. I also coached football at Avondale High School for twenty-four years. One of my favorite mottos was, "What you give, you have. What you didn't give, you have lost forever!" I can remember talking to Carl in 1982 about football and life. Carl wasn't a starter on the team but he was a young man that gave his very best on every play in practice and in games. I wanted Carl to know how I appreciated his attitude, work ethic, and perseverance. Our team was made better because of him. I also knew these traits would make Carl a better man in his life endeavors. It is a pleasure to know that Carl's calling to God has made that motto true. "What you give, you have..." Carl, I hope these words fully express my love for you and what you are doing for our world.

Coach Richard Brewer
Avondale School District
Detroit, MI

I am extremely excited and proud of my spiritual son in the Gospel whom I had the opportunity to Pastor for several years. I believe that all that read this book will open themselves to experience the supernatural power of the Holy Ghost operating in Apostle Carl Flowers' life and ministry. Surely, he has been a dedicated soldier and servant of our Lord and Savior Jesus Christ. I have seen personally through Apostle Carl Flowers that if a man or woman will commit their life to Christ, that their life could experience a great transformation. My prayer is that Apostle Carl Flowers and those that read this book will be blessed and highly favored of the Lord.

Apostle Jimmy Peters
Peters Memorial Ministries
Poplarville, MS

Over the last twenty years I have met many preachers, teachers, reverends and evangelist but rarely do I meet a TRUE "Front Line Soldier" in the Army of God. I mean, a man who straps on his Spiritual Armor every single morning of his life and walks to the front line to fight the "good fight of Faith" for Jesus Christ. Carl Flowers is such a man. A man who sets the shining example for others "cut from the same cloth" of what real "go ye therefore" Ministry looks like. Carl Flowers is one of those rare men that is not afraid to look into the eyes of broken, hurting, hopeless and desperate people. He is one of those rare men that will not look the other way when confronted by the things of Hell because he has already lived through them - Yet, came out on the other side victorious in Christ Jesus. Carl Flowers is a walking living testimony and Spiritual Hero to all those who have found themselves being caught up and destroyed by the scourge of Drug Addiction. I urge you to not only read but digest the Godly wisdom Carl Flowers is about to share with you in this book. He is placing his heart on the table for all to see for the Glory of Jesus Christ. Revelation 12: 11 tells us that "we overcome him {Satan} by the blood of the Lamb and by the Word of our testimony; and that we should not love our lives so much as to shrink from death {in our service to God}. Carl Flowers is a man who has determined to live by that scripture every day of his life. If you are broken or have a heart for the broken – THIS testimony was written for you.

Pastor Charlie Haynes
Founder of Jacob's Well Recovery Center for Women
And Damascus Road Recovery Center for Men
Pearl River County, Mississippi

Carl Flowers... A man that has been in bondage. A man that that has chosen to be free in Christ. A man that has the testimony to back up his story. A man that is leading others in bondage to freedom through the love of King Jesus. Yes this man is truly a freedom fighter in the Kingdom. Read this book, listen to this warrior of love's heart and let these words challenge you to become a disciple of deliverance.

Pastor Clarence Tilghman
Director of Damascus Road Recovery Center for Men
Poplarville, MS

Honored and blessed, words that epitomize how I feel about knowing Apostle Carl Flowers, a man who I firmly believe is an angel sent directly from heaven for such a time as this. I am in awe of his humility as he reaches thousands with the Gospel of Jesus Christ. Carl Flowers is a man who has been called to raise up Christian leaders and show them the way to go and how to withstand the daily beatings of the enemy while fighting on the front lines of battles unseen. Coming out of my own addiction and struggles, I am forever grateful to know that I am not alone, and it is because of men of honor like this man of God that I am who I am today, for he walked this out ahead of me and was able to show me the way through his own story.

Julie Keene
Author of #JWGirl4Life – Where the Light Meets the Dark
Picayune, MS

FROM SIN & SHAME TO GLORY

Table of Contents

My struggle with addiction brought about my conversion to Jesus Christ as Lord and Savior over my life. I was originally a dead person, a sinner in God's sight. I had neither position nor possessions before me, nor the power to stay free from addiction during this battle. But I have obtained something real, the reality that I am a new being, a person made new through the blood of Jesus Christ.

Chapter One
The Sin of Addiction
(The Root of the Problem)
Fact of Sin

If we are to hope for change and see true deliverance in our personal lives, we must begin to troubleshoot and get to the root of the problem. We have to accept the responsibilities of past, present, and future mistakes.

The parable of the lawnmower

I love to mow grass; I find it quite therapeutic. I love the smell of fresh cut grass. I love to see sidewalks edged, the bushes trimmed, the flowers blooming in their tropical landscapes, palm trees blowing in the wind. It gives any home that sought after "curb appeal". A well maintained landscape also gives insight to who lives in the home. In order to complete the process of a well-manicured lawn, we need the right tools! We need a lawn mower with sharp blades, the hedge trimmer must have the proper trim, and a wheelbarrow ready to haul dirt is a must have. To complete the process, we need the proper man-power to operate the equipment. The oil would need to be checked. And who could forget gas in the motor? Most importantly we must be determined to see it to completion. Faith without works is dead.

One day, I went out to mow the grass, but this day there was something amiss. The lawn mower was not operating properly. It would not work and I could not get it started. Normally, I would take it to a small engine shop to resolve the issue, but this day I was determined to troubleshoot the problem alone. In doing so, I went through each meticulous step, pinpointing everything on the mower that causes the motor not to run. I checked the oil, the gas, the spark plug. I looked under the mower to see if the blade assembly was free. The major problem I found, was the pull string wouldn't come out so I thought something major had happened. I thought maybe the motor was locked up. I was so frustrated! The lawnmower in question is a commercial machine, I had owned it for a long time, I took good care it, but for some strange reason, it would not start. Something was wrong. With that being said, I began to take the entire thing apart, determined to find the cause of its disrepair. I pulled the spring assembly apart, took out the spark plug, and changed the oil. As I began to reassemble the lawnmower, I felt important. I was going to fix this problem, and in doing so, I found out more about the lawnmower than I had ever known before. With the initiative to do it myself and the proper tools, I fixed the problem and was on my way to a clean cut lawn.

As Christians, we must stay in operation! In order to do so, we must know how to troubleshoot so we can stay on the "cutting-edge"! I find this to be the latest and most advanced stage in the development of someone or something. Confession is made unto salvation, but studying and living the word of God will keep our souls well-manicured. The word of God, the Bible, is the instruction manual of Christian living. It is, what I like to refer to, as "Basic Instructions Before Leaving Earth."

All scripture is given by inspiration of God, and is profitable for doctrine, for reproof, for correction, for instruction in righteousness.
2Tim 3:16

The truth and operation of Jesus Christ as the Word troubleshoots any problems that may occur. The difference in this parable is that He can fix *everything* that we get ourselves into and He will allow us to troubleshoot every area of our lives so that we may live in total submission to Him.

Have you checked your oil today? Even if you have a good running lawnmower, it must be used correctly. In order for the line to look good, it has to be done in proper sequence. You cannot mow the lawn without weed-eating. You cannot grow flowers without proper fertilization and the right amount of water. You cannot trim the tree without the trimmer. The process cannot be enjoyed without the work, without taking the *initiative* to push for results. When all is done, you can sit down in the shade and enjoy the fruit of your labor in love.

Like in every tree and in every plant, every problem has its roots.

I was born and raised in Michigan, in a single-parent household with a loving and hard-working mother who did very her best to provide for my brother and I. She did so by working to clean other people's homes, by washing dishes in a restaurant for two dollars an hour, then coming home to make sure we are taken care of. We were raised in a very loving environment. Christmas was a very exciting time for my family. We enjoyed the snowy days and were elated at the expectation of gifts under the tree. The feast took an entire week to prepare. My mother put her whole heart and time into making sure that we were happy. She never ruined the "Santa Claus" surprise for us, we had to find that out on our own.

I remember one Christmas like it was yesterday. It was late in the morning, close to 3:00AM. My mom was struggling to put together a bicycle, poring over instructions, using the tools that made a lot of racket. I was anxiously awakened by her parents, my grandparents, so that I might catch a glimpse of Santa Claus; however, I was met by the determination on my mother's face. Her desire was to everything right for her boy's Christmas morning surprise. As I took a peek around the corner and down the hallway, she turned with a glimpse and with her radiant smile, told me to come help her. I was so excited and in my jubilation, I ran down the hall to see all the toys already exposed under the tree. Although I had forgotten my glasses in all my excitement and could not see all that well, my eyes were open to who Santa Claus *really* was. We were happy with it all, even though most of our toys throughout the year came out of the Tide box, Cracker Jack box, or the cereal box...except for Christmas morning.

I was born in 1964 around the time of the Vietnam War. My mother married my father in 1963, after leaving a life of poverty and a womanizing military man from Chicago. She never looked back as she migrated out of the southern blazing heat in Columbia, MS, leaving my oldest brother, Jessie, behind with her parents. She traded the sweltering summers for the snowy suburbs of Michigan. She was determined just to help us grow into a new life where Motown Records were spitting out singing sensations and crooning from the radio came tunes from the Temptations such as "The Way You Do the Things You Do". The Supremes broke records with "Baby Love" and the Beatles were topping charts with "I Wanna Hold Your Hand". And who could forget that tune by the Drifters, "Under the Boardwalk"? Elvis Presley was a national hit with "Kissing Cousins and Mary Wells sang topped it off with "My Guy", also at Motown Records.

You can imagine the life of the city that surrounded my conception, shortly after the assassination of our 35th President in Dallas, TX on November 22nd, 1963, President John F. Kennedy. America was engaged in a long battle and costly war in Vietnam and my family lost one of their own, Staff Sergeant Willy James McLaurin, my uncle, who was awarded not only the Medal of Honor, but the National Defense Service Medal, the Vietnam Campaign Medal, and the Purple

Heart for serving his country faithfully during two tours in the Vietnam War, losing his battle and his life to hostile wounds from an explosive device. My heroic uncle was named a ground casualty in Kein Hoa Province, South Vietnam in 1970.

At the time of my birth 1964, Martin Luther King, Jr. was awarded the Nobel Peace Prize and was the first person in the Western world to have shown us that a struggle can be waged without violence. Martin Luther King, Jr. was the first to make the message of brotherly love a reality. In the course of his public struggle, he brought that very message to all men, all nations, and all races. Martin Luther King's dream was that all inhabitants of the United States would be judged by their personal qualities and not by the color of their skin. In April 1968 he was murdered by a white racist. Four years earlier, he had received the Peace Prize for his nonviolent campaign against racism.

The culture was in disarray, engaged in war while President Lyndon Johnson called for the country to unite. All the while, on June 21, 1964, the great state of Mississippi was at war, too. Andy Goodman and two other civil rights workers, James Chaney and Michael Schwerner, were ambushed and shot dead by the Klu Klux Klan in Philadelphia, MS and their bodies were found in an earth dam in rural Neshoba County, an entire 44 days after their disappearance. The rest of Mississippi was burning in murders.

Black people had all already shown they were ready to fight in any war. One million had joined the armed forces during World War II. But despite military desegregation in 1948, another decade would pass before it actually came to pass. It was the same across civilian life. In 1954, it was reported around the globe that America had outlawed segregation and in 1955, the Supreme Court said that segregated education should end. However, ten years later, more than 75% of school districts remained segregated and one half the black population was living below the poverty line.

Slavery still exists.

Slavery still exists. Only this time it is a choice made in free will. We voluntarily enslave ourselves when we indulge in the bondage of sin to include alcohol, drugs, sex, and the like. Any addiction is a by-product of sin. Hate is also a by-product of sin.

Racism is a sin. The bible says,
Everyone who sins is breaking God's law, for all sin is contrary to the law of God."
1 John 3:4

Love is a by-product of the nature of God.

God loved the world so much that he gave his one and only Son, so that everyone who believes in him will not perish but have eternal life.
John 3:16

But if you show favoritism, you sin and are convicted by the law as lawbreakers. For whoever keeps the whole law and yet stumbles at just one point is guilty of breaking all of it. For he who said, "You shall not commit adultery," also said, "You shall not murder." If you do not commit adultery but do commit murder, you have become a lawbreaker.
James 2:9-11

When people choose to love or to hate, it is predicated on the condition of their heart.

We know that our old man was crucified with him so that the body of sin would no longer dominate us, so that we would no longer be enslaved to sin.
Romans 6:6

The quickest way to become a slave to sin is to practice something that is habit forming and destructive. Over eating, gambling, sex, pornography, television, social media, video games, and even prescription medication will put you on a roller coaster ride of destructive behavior.

We do it to ourselves.

Self-inflicted wounds.

Harming oneself.

ALL of these are just a by-product of SIN.

Solomon says it best.

A city broken into [and] left without a wall, [so] is a person who lacks self-control.
Proverbs 25:28

In 1966, my mother was going through an emotional separation with my father. I had not even made it to my second birthday. My father could not let the streets go. He beat a Murder charge by claiming self-defense while gambling in the night clubs in Pontiac, Michigan.

My mother, the oldest of ten siblings is a survivor. She continued to seek the Lord, praying, sacrificing of herself, living in the basement of her younger sister's home. She was determined to make it. She was blessed with a career in the auto industry working for GMC and was able to retire from that job. Growing up, we had no idea that we were poor. My mother did the best she could in raising us. We had shelter, food and all the necessities of life...nothing more...nothing less. She gave us her love daily; it was all the love we could ever ask for. Her teachings were based on the Bible. Her favorite saying was, "Cleanliness is next to Godliness." My mother was active in the church and worked long hours which afforded her the opportunity to purchase our first home on the east side of Pontiac. We were finally off welfare and out of the projects. You might guess that I am, in fact, a die-hard Detroit Lions fan!

As a child there were a lot of things to get involved in around our neighborhood. We saw a lot of debauchery daily to include murder, drug infestations, anything you could imagine. Even though there was no one in my life influencing me negatively, I still drifted in the wrong direction by choice. I believe a lot of things contributed to that factor. I even used the excuse of not having my father with me in our home, but that was just an excuse. My uncle Sonny, a police officer, even lived with us. I respected him very much. He stepped in as disciplinary alongside my mother and helped through the crisis of my youth. I believe I would have been a lot worse off if he had not come in on occasion to correct me on some of the things I would get caught doing.

I progressively got worse in the Pontiac school system where I tried to blend in with the worst of the crowds and indulged in marijuana, alcohol, sex, and in fighting every threat that came my way. These things eventually caused my expulsion from school for poor behavior.

In 1978 I was sent off to Piney Woods Country Life School. The Piney Woods Country Life School was a co-educational African American independent boarding school located 21 miles south of Jackson, Mississippi in Rankin County, 900 miles from home. I packed up all my problems which would eventually explode, got into an altercation on this new campus, and was expelled and sent right back home.

My next move was to get back into school in Auburn Heights, Michigan. I would have to attend Avondale

Middle School because at the time I was behind and needed to attend eighth-grade all over again. This turned out to be for my good. I began to take an interest in sports, playing football and running track. I became preoccupied with sports and learned through that to develop healthier relationships. It was the coaches, Ray Went and Richard (Rhino) Brewer, who helped me to stay disciplined. Coach Brewer motivated me one day after a big game we lost, one I wasn't allowed to start in. He must have seen that I was feeling a certain kind of way, so he came to me saying, "Carl! One day, you will be a better man." Then he went on to commend me on my work ethics.

I began to make new friends quickly after that and what a blessing considering I had a limited black culture mind-set that I had developed from the street life. I was raised to love everyone, but I had heard and experienced prejudice and racism, two things not tolerated in my family. As I moved to a predominantly white school, I learned to appreciate the experience of making new friends in a new culture, friends I still have in my life today.

For the most part, I settled down and progressed in not only sports and grades (which were just good enough to pass) throughout my high school years. Soon after graduation in 1983, I enlisted in the United States Army and began basic training in Fort Jackson, South Carolina. It wasn't long before my heart was broken and my dreams shattered as I was released on medical discharge for my bad eyesight.

It was a huge disappointment for me, returning to Pontiac, Michigan to an atmosphere of addiction, drinking, snorting cocaine, freebasing crack cocaine, going to after-hours clubs in Detroit, blowing money at the adult bars in Windsor, Ontario and bouncing from one house party after another. l loved my mixture of music such as "Beat It" by Michael Jackson, "Don't Stop Believin'" by Journey, "Welcome to the Jungle" by Guns N Roses, "Another One Bites the Dust" by Queen, "You Shook Me All Night Long" by AC/DC and of course who could forget those 80's and 90's Rap hits – "Fight The Power" by Public Enemy, "Push It" by Salt 'N Pepa, "My Adidas" by Run-DMC, "Self-Destruction" by Stop The Violence Movement, "Wild Thing" by Tone Loc, "Bite It" by UTFO and "I'm Bad" by LL Cool J. Influential beats and lyrics of songs is an open door to the heart of the soul. The cultural impact of music plays an influencing role in America, good or bad. Teenagers today listen to an average of nearly 2.5 hours of music per day. Guess what they are hearing about?

One in three popular songs contains explicit references to drug or alcohol use, and lust is entering into the gates of your ears.

I was listening to loud music intoxicated when I received a DUI driving the wrong way down a snowy street in Michigan.

Things did not get much better for me until 1986, when I moved back to Mississippi following the news that my grandfather was dying of cancer. Keep in mind I still was struggling with my addictions. I ended up staying in Mississippi with my grandmother, working in grocery stores, and working at an ammunition plant at NASA's Stennis Space Center.

I can vaguely remember different details within episodes of my early life, the highlights if you will, when my problems began. In writing this, I believe it is important to get to the point and to the root of the problem when I hopped on the roller coaster of sin to include substance abuse, pornography, and isolation in the terror of sinful nature which was like a metastatic cancer spreading into my adulthood.

My addiction started at the ripe old age of 12 when I was looking for acceptance and trying to find myself and where I fit in with others. Since I was not really focused on school, I retrogressed into areas of entrapment. I fell into sin.

Being kicked out of school for drinking, fighting, etc. at such an early age was evidence that I had a problem. I was a very introverted person, quiet. But deep down inside I wanted to express myself and become more like some of my family members and friends. I can remember drinking at a very early age, going to school drunk off my stepfather's liquor. I don't know what it was I believed. I'm sure I had a complex about my eyesight and having to wear glasses at such a young age. I guess I thought I didn't look as good as everyone else. I can remember getting teased and being called, "Four-Eyes" and "Mr. Pee-Body". People had me feeling a certain kind of way with all that name-calling, even though I was NOT a nerd, I sure did look like one. This was a big contributing factor for me not being able to open up to anyone to discuss my insecurities.

I was a totally different person when I would indulge in drinking alcohol. I tried to smoke cigarettes at a young age and got caught and disciplined by my uncle who sat me down and made me smoke a whole pack of cool menthols. I literally got high off the cigarettes that day. After that little disciplinary method, my uncle and I never smoked another cigarette or should I say I did not develop a habit of smoking cigarettes. The alcohol was a completely different story. It made me open to communication; however, I could not just stop at one or two drinks. I sought out the feeling and began to abuse it just so I *could* communicate and feel accepted. As soon as I would sober up, I would become completely silent again. I had problems expressing myself and could not open up to anyone but my mother. I felt justified since I had no father in my life and all I knew of my father was that he was an alcoholic and loved to party so I begin taking on those traits. At that age I was surely interested in girls, but could not express myself like my brothers and uncles were able to. I was shy, wanting to talk and wanting to share, but soon satan opened the gates of my eyes to a whole new addiction and I found myself bound by lust.

I remember a time in particular, I was very young and two very promiscuous sisters in the neighborhood stripped off my clothes behind their house. They were much older than me and that had me feeling a certain kind of way. I couldn't have been no more than 10 years old and still very much a virgin. I didn't know *what* to do. One day, my curiosity got the best of me when I stumbled across one of my stepfather's pornography magazines. This began an addiction, a personal stronghold that satan used to destroy personal relationships throughout the remainder of my life as a young adult. It only added to my isolated shame. So, now, not only did I have an alcohol problem, a problem with communication, a problem not being able to talk to girls, but now I wanted to have sex with those girls and I didn't even know the basics of how a relationship worked. I was doomed to this stronghold of lust, wanting nothing more than to skip every base and just have sex with whomever, whenever. My life was a struggle to say the least.

My addictions didn't start the first time I drank alcohol, indulged in drugs or even had sex, it all stemmed from the root of Sin .

So you may be asking, "How did this start?"

The Bible explains the origin in the beginning.

Behold, I was shapen in iniquity; and in sin did my
mother conceive me.
Psalm 51:5

Sin will take you farther than you want to go, keep
you longer than you want to stay, and cost you more
than you want to pay.

The Fact of Sin

In order to truly have a stronger relationship with
God, we must repent of our problems by applying
ourselves to Gods word.

And that from childhood you have known the Holy
Scriptures, which are able to make you wise for
salvation through faith which is in Christ Jesus.
2 Tim 3:15

My problems came in my youth and I had never been
rooted and grounded in the Word of God, even
though I attended my Baptist Church regularly. I was
amused by the choir, I did not fully understand many
sermons, but down in my heart I knew there was a
god. I heard many stories of Jesus but I did not *know*
Him as my Lord and Savior. I had religion with no
relationship. I dressed up, went to church, even was
baptized in the midst of my sin, but I never fully
understood or grasped what I was doing at the time.
With that being said, I know when and why my
problems started. I would sing the tune, "Jesus loves
me, this I know, for the Bible tells me so", but I failed
to live a true life in Jesus Christ. This, in turn, led to

my entanglement with sin and the journey of
addiction began.

In order to truly have a stronger relationship with
Christ, we must repent.

*Whosoever committed sin transgresseth also the
law: for sin is the transgression of the law.*
1 John 3:4

*For the wages of sin is death, but the free gift of God
is eternal life in Christ Jesus our Lord.*
Romans 6:23

*Therefore, just as sin came into the world through
one man, and death through sin, and so death
spread to all men because all sinned.*
Romans 5:12

*Don't you know that when you yourself to someone
or something as obedient slaves, your or slaves of
the of the one you obey--whether you are slaves to
sin, which leads to death, or to obedience, which
leads to righteousness?*
Romans 6:16

In my old neighborhoods in Michigan, from Pontiac
to Detroit to Auburn Hills, there was so much to do
that could make you or break you. Unfortunately, I
chose the life of the streets. By God's Grace I escaped
death on more than one occasion. I was saved and
given the opportunity to capitalize on my mistake
through Jesus Christ. I pray this book will be a

blessing to someone who had similar life experiences with sin and shame, but now you are looking to Jesus Christ to bring you to the GLORY!

I soon settled in Picayune, Mississippi. I found myself living with my grandma and dealing with unresolved personal issues. My life came to a crashing halt when I was overcome by a debilitating crack addiction. I had *some* girlfriends (I guess you could call them "sex buddies") that had me also deep into lustful relationships that came to dead ends

The Glory

The Glory didn't come until I got in a serious relationship with Jesus Christ. During the transition of my conversion, I was introduced to my soul mate, my wife. She was beginning a career in, you guessed it, Law Enforcement and I started using drugs undercover. satan had me bound. I guess you can imagine that the relationship was on the rocks. I could not hide anymore when the beast came to the surface. I would try desperately to cover it up but it always showed up. Relapse after relapse came and went. The sin of crack cocaine had empowered me and began to destroy the image of God that I was created to be. I was exposed, I felt the shame, and I LIVED the shame.

Things did not change until I finally surrendered to Jesus Christ who delivered me. I had been relying on my own feelings and experiences and I felt constantly defeated trying to quit on my own. I shed so many tears due to this bondage of addiction. If anyone relies on his own feelings as an instrument, he will constantly be defeated. But if he sees the fact that his co-death with Christ, that person will be set free. I started a new family and life with my wife of now 30 years. We have two beautiful children from our union.

For a man indeed ought not to cover his head, since he is the image and glory of God; but woman is the glory of man. For man is not from woman, but woman from man. Nor was man created for the woman, but woman for the man.
1 Corinthians 11:7-9 (KJV)

God connected us and I developed true genuine feelings for her, but I still had the cancer of my addiction in the closet. It soon came out and knocked me on my knees seeking true deliverance in Jesus name.

In 1993, I truly accepted Jesus Christ as my Lord and Savior. God not only saved me, He also saved my wife who was contemplating suicide because of our problems. The Lord led us to a small church in Poplarville, Mississippi, Peters Memorial Church of God in Christ under the leadership of Apostle Jimmy Peters. This is where the glory began. Even as a new believer, I still had several relapses in my addiction but as I totally surrendered myself, Christ called me to ministry. This relationship with Christ brought deliverance after several relapses, increased my faith in the Lord, and I became a Pastor. I will have been completely free from my old self 23 years in October 2016. To God be the Glory!

Chapter Two
The Shame of Addiction
Fact of Separation

Fact of separation - Sin separates us from God.

Behold, the LORD'S hand is not shortened, that it cannot save; neither his ear heavy, that it cannot hear: But your iniquities have separated between you and your God, and your sins have hid his face from you, that he will not hear.
Isaiah 59:1-2

For the wages of sin is death; but the gift of God is eternal life through Jesus Christ our Lord.
Romans 6:23

But if ye will not do so, behold, ye have sinned against the LORD: and be sure your sin will find you out.
Numbers 32:23

In order to truly have a stronger relationship with Jesus Christ, we must confess our problem with sin... If we confess our sins, he is faithful and just to forgive us our sins, and to cleanse us from all unrighteousness.
1 John 1:9

Sin has addictive qualities and works to try to destroy our relationship with the Lord - and our families.

Addiction is a strong urge or craving to repeat a behavior regardless of its consequences.

The person who is addicted has lost control of their behavior.

A Look at Drug Addiction

It wasn't until I could really look at myself to actually see the retrogression. As I stated in Chapter One, after 20 years on the roller coaster ride of addiction, I bottomed out and flat-lined in spiritual death! My sin was exposed by my appearance as well as by my spirit. When the Holy Spirit comes into our lives, we then progress with healthy habits such as spending time with family, being more productive on our jobs, loving people, and most importantly...loving ourselves. The bottom line is, we cannot hide sin. It will be exposed. The Word of God is our life-line. If we don't take heed to it, the Bible states clearly what will happen:

But if ye will not do so, behold, ye have sinned against the LORD: and be sure your sin will find you out.
Numbers 32:23

- The addicted person repeats the behavior regardless of consequences

- The drug is in control (the person is enslaved by the drug)

- It starts out as fun, but eventually the drug begins to destroy the addicts' life

- It becomes very difficult to break the "hold" that the drug has on the addict

- The urge for the drug is so strong that the addict will betray loved ones to get it

- Some addicts are able to quit using for a while, but most of them eventually repeat the behavior again, regardless of the consequences

A Look at Sin - Disobedience to God's Law

At some point, we must realize that we have gotten way off track and the direction we are going in is absolutely destructive and we are soon to flat-line. Everything connected to us is now infected because of our addictive behavior and disobedience. There is no trust. I didn't even trust myself. I was disobedient to what I truly believed and who I truly believed IN. My life had become unmanageable and at this point, I was not fit to live *or* fit to die. Disobedience is the same as witchcraft.

- Sinners repeat the behavior regardless of consequences

- Sin is in control (the person enslaved by sin)

- Starts out as fun, but eventually sin begins to destroy the sinners' life

- It becomes very difficult to break the "hold" that sin has on the sinner

- The urge for the sin is so strong that the sinner will betray loved ones and even God for it

- Some sinners are able to quit sinning for a while, but most of them eventually repeat the behavior again, regardless of the consequences

Addiction to drugs and the constant urge and failure to stop sinning have very similar qualities.

Is it possible to be addicted to SIN?

Repentance is to acknowledge wrongdoing. It is a decision to turn AWAY from sin and turn TO God for forgiveness. Have you truly repented and asked for forgiveness from God then run right back to the same sin? Why can't we just leave sin alone?

SIN IS POWERFUL

Genesis 3:1-13 - Now the serpent was more crafty than any of the wild animals the LORD God had made. He said to the woman, "Did God really say, 'You must not eat from any tree in the garden'?"
2 The woman said to the serpent, "We may eat fruit from the trees in the garden, 3 but God did say, 'You must not eat fruit from the tree that is in the middle of the garden, and you must not touch it, or you will die.'"

4 "You will not certainly die," the serpent said to the woman. 5 "For God knows that when you eat from it your eyes will be opened, and you will be like God, knowing good and evil."

6 When the woman saw that the fruit of the tree was good for food and pleasing to the eye, and also desirable for gaining wisdom, she took some and ate it. She also gave some to her husband, who was with her, and he ate it. 7 Then the eyes of both of them were opened, and they realized they were naked; so they sewed fig leaves together and made coverings for themselves.

8 Then the man and his wife heard the sound of the LORD God as he was walking in the garden in the cool of the day, and they hid from the LORD God among the trees of the garden. 9 But the LORD God called to the man, "Where are you?"

10 He answered, "I heard you in the garden, and I was afraid because I was naked; so I hid."

11 And he said, "Who told you that you were naked? Have you eaten from the tree that I commanded you not to eat from?"

12 The man said, "The woman you put here with me— she gave me some fruit from the tree, and I ate it."

13 Then the LORD God said to the woman, "What is this you have done?"

The woman said, "The serpent deceived me, and I ate."

Describe some of the qualities of sin that you see in the story of Adam, Eve and the serpent.

_____
_____
_____
_____
_____
_____
_____
_____
_____
_____
_____
_____
_____
_____
_____
_____

Adam, Eve and the serpent - Characteristics of Sin

- Sin is desirable
- Sin is pleasing to the eye
- Sin fulfills a need
- Sin is attractive
- Sin is deceptive

- Sin is dangerous
- Sin separates us from God
- Sin is deadly

But your iniquities have separated between you and your God, and your sins have hid his face from you, that he will not hear.
Isaiah 59:2

Adam and Eve have been made aware of the terrible consequences of disobeying God, yet they continue to sin. Sounds a lot like us doesn't it?

Why do we sin when we know there are bad consequences when we disobey God?

_____

_____

_____

_____

_____

_____

_____

_____

Now the works of the flesh are manifest, which are these; Adultery, fornication, uncleanness, lasciviousness, Idolatry, witchcraft, hatred, variance, emulations, wrath, strife, seditions, heresies, Envyings, murders, drunkenness, revellings, and such like: of the which I tell you

before, as I have also told you in time past, that they which do such things shall not inherit the kingdom of God. But the fruit of the Spirit is love, joy, peace, longsuffering, gentleness, goodness, faith, Meekness, temperance: against such there is no law. And they that are Christ's have crucified the flesh with the affections and lusts.
Galatians 5: 19-24

HOW SIN ATTACKS US

Let no man say when he is tempted, I am tempted of God: for God cannot be tempted with evil, neither tempteth he any man: But every man is tempted, when he is drawn away of his own lust, and enticed. Then when lust hath conceived, it bringeth forth sin: and sin, when it is finished, bringeth forth death.
James 1: 13-15

- Desire leads to Sin

- Sin grows...Sin grows...Sin grows out of control

- Full-Grown, Out of control sin then leads to Death

Things we tell ourselves

- "I am still in control, I can stop this sin if I really try."

- "God knows my heart. He knows that I am just flesh."

- "The Devil made me do it."

- "I'll get it together and repent soon."

- "This is not hurting anybody."

- "I'll stop this sin before it does me any harm."

- "God will forgive me."

Paul's Honesty

I do not understand what I do. For what I want to do I do not do, but what I hate I do. ¹⁶ And if I do what I do not want to do, I agree that the law is good. ¹⁷ As it is, it is no longer I myself who do it, but it is sin living in me. ¹⁸ For I know that good itself does not dwell in me, that is, in my sinful nature. For I have the desire to do what is good, but I cannot carry it out. ¹⁹ For I do not do the good I want to do, but the evil I do not want to do—this I keep on doing. ²⁰ Now if I do what I do not want to do, it is no longer I who do it, but it is sin living in me that does it.
²¹ So I find this law at work: Although I want to do good, evil is right there with me. ²² For in my inner being I delight in God's law; ²³ but I see another law at work in me, waging war against the law of my mind and making me a prisoner of the law of sin at work within me. ²⁴ What a wretched man I am! Who will rescue me from this body that is subject to

death? ²⁵ *Thanks be to God, who delivers me through Jesus Christ our Lord!*
So then, I myself in my mind am a slave to God's law, but in my sinful nature a slave to the law of sin.
Romans 7: 15-25

What is Paul going through?

_____
_____
_____
_____
_____
_____
_____

Can you relate to his struggle with sin? How?

_____
_____
_____
_____
_____
_____
_____

Paul is honest about his struggle with sin. Paul admits that there is "evil" in his life.

Therefore, in order to keep me from becoming conceited, I was given a thorn in my flesh, a messenger of Satan, to torment me. ⁸ Three times I pleaded with the Lord to take it away from me. ⁹ But he said to me, "My grace is sufficient for you, for my power is made perfect in weakness." Therefore I will boast all the more gladly about my weaknesses, so that Christ's power may rest on me. ¹⁰ That is why, for Christ's sake, I delight in weaknesses, in insults, in hardships, in persecutions, in difficulties. For when I am weak, then I am strong.
II Corinthians 12: 7-10

Paul pleaded for the thorn to be removed. Many bible scholars believe the thorn represents temptation. What does the Lord's response tell us about sin?

_____
_____
_____
_____
_____
_____
_____
_____

What message is being sent to us concerning our weaknesses?

_____

_____

_____

_____

_____

_____

_____

Why do we have to deal with sin? Because sin has a purpose!!

- Our battle against sin causes us to rely on God. Only through our relationship with God can we defeat sin.

- Sin creates opportunities for God to see our allegiance to Him. We are forced to choose between God and sin. God is pleased when we choose Him.

- Sin separates the children of God from the children of the Devil and allows God to judge us. Those who are faithful to God will receive heaven as their reward.

- The Devil uses sin to try to destroy our lives. In the end, the Lord will be victorious. But we must endure the test to the end.

Have you *truly* repented if you go back to the same sin?

Jesus said to his disciples: "Things that cause people to stumble are bound to come, but woe to anyone through whom they come. ² It would be better for them to be thrown into the sea with a millstone tied around their neck than to cause one of these little ones to stumble. ³ So watch yourselves.
"If your brother or sister sins against you, rebuke them; and if they repent, forgive them. ⁴ Even if they sin against you seven times in a day and seven times come back to you saying 'I repent,' you must forgive them."
Luke 17:1-4

What does God's standard for repentance in this scripture tell us?

_____
_____
_____
_____
_____
_____
_____
_____

There will be times when we fall short and sin against God's law.

If we deliberately keep on sinning after we have received the knowledge of the truth, no sacrifice for sins is left.
Hebrews 10:26

Don't take advantage of grace. It is there when you need it, but it is not to be misused. God does expect us to live a Godly life.

Successful strategies in managing sin

How can the Christian more effectively manage and avoid sin?

_____
_____
_____
_____
_____
_____
_____
_____

What has worked for you?

_____
_____

_____

_____

_____

_____

_____

_____

Some things you can do

- Admit that you have a problem and that you need God's help to deal with it.

- Eliminate the clutter (bad people, bad influences) in your life.

- Clean house of things that remind you of your addiction such as paraphernalia, books, pictures, etc.

- Develop closer relationships with other Christians.

- Get a spiritual father, a prayer partner.

- Stay in the Word.

- Come to Church. Show up, grow up and go on.

- FLEE from situations that might cause you to sin.

- PRAY and ask God for the strength to resist sin.

- If you haven't tried it yet...DON'T! You just might like it...and if you like it, you could get addicted to it.

The Ultimate Goal is to OVERCOME SIN

He that hath an ear, let him hear what the Spirit saith unto the churches; to him that overcometh will I give to eat of the tree of life, which is in the midst of the paradise of God.
Revelation 2:7

Everyone makes mistakes; some are more serious and lead to death and some not so serious. The greatest mistake is in thinking we can get away with sin, thinking that we cannot win, and breaking fellowship with God.

We were created to fellowship with God, in the Garden of Eden, walking and talking with God. It was our sin that halted that fellowship. It brings about a lack of assurance. Sin robs us of the joy of the Lord. It keeps our prayers from being answered. SIN IS SERIOUS.

We need to consider how serious it is when we are tempted. Seeing what effects it has our own families, we can't help but be held responsible, for they reap the consequences of our sin as well. Our loved ones suffer because of our sin. The sins of Adam and Eve affected *all* of their descendants, including you and

me. David's sins caused the child's death. Children affected by the sins of the parents and parents are affected by the sins of the children. Husbands and wives are affected by the sins of their spouses.

Sin also affects you physically. In the Bible, some at the church in Corinth became ill and died due to their sin. Sin also brings chastising. Many acts of sin brings about our own judgement here on earth because what we sow we will also reap in the flesh. SIN WILL AFFECT YOU FOREVER.

Sadly, sin affects the service and costs us our Christian rewards. The good news is that sin can be forgiven. Jesus Christ died for our sin. Receiving Jesus Christ as our Lord and Savior makes us justified. I have more good news! Believers can live victorious and in abundant living we can walk in that victory daily in Jesus Name!

Preaching Nuggets for the Exhortation

There is a demonic attack by every wicked spirit, but now I have power and dominion over every power and personality that comes my way. God has given us the authority. He said whatever is bound on earth shall be bound in heaven. He give us the keys to the Kingdom of God. He tells us seek first the kingdom of God in His righteousness then He said all these things should be added unto us.

Beloved, we have a great life in Christ, if we can only pursue Him by seeking Him. This is a prayer devotion, a prayer school, Amen. You can call it the first grade of prayer. I'm not trying to be deep right now. I am trying to get your heart open to seek and receive God. He said you seek Him you will find Him, you call on Him he will come near to you. This is the type of God who knows your voice.

A lot of times we ask other people to pray for us but we can't leave our concerns and needs in the hands of other people. It's time for you to seek God and cry out to be a better you. Tell him about your future, tell Him about your deepest heart desires, and tell Him how much you love Him. He KNOWS all of it, Amen! Praise God! He knows that the life you lived in the past *was* your past, Amen! He cast all your sins as far as the east is from the west and he loads you up daily with benefits of your salvation.

Today is a new day, this is a new season. God said there is a new you, a greater you inside. I come to encourage you beloved if only you would cry out to God daily. Make prayer a habit. I cannot emphasis enough that prayer was the most important process of me being elevated by the Holy Spirit. My Pastor began to see the spirit of prayer on me, he allowed me to pray for people, and he even allowed me to open up the prayer services. I would go in and pray privately when no one else was present to hear me and I would pour out my heart before the Lord. I would fast and pray. Temptation would come and even through times of trials and errors I would fail at different things. Life is a roller coaster of highs and lows and somedays I would lose. However, I would get back up on my feet. I would pray and confess my sins and ask God to forgive me. I would walk out of condemnation and walk right into victory through the power of prayer.

There is HOPE! There is hope to everyone going through rough patches. There is hope to the family is distress. There is hope for the one being destroyed by the devices of wickedness. No weapon formed against you shall prosper, my beloved, because God is building you up with the Word. We are going to go through this process. We are going to begin to walk in victory by the power of prayer. We are going to begin to decree and declare that we are not turning back, AMEN! We are not going back to the place from which we came. If anything, we are pressing forward toward tomorrow to the prize of the high calling. We KNOW what the low calling is. We have been there! We have been in the darkness, we have been through the valley of the shadow of death. Now we are walking to the hills!

Let me tell you something, the lower the low the higher the high, so may your heart be encouraged by knowing that a Spirit that is greater is inside of you! God is going to bring you to victory. God is going to see you praying without ceasing. God is going to build you up!

A lot of times we are torn down due the sin of the world, but when you get in the presence of God, He will begin to give you strength and the inward man will then have the power to prevail! The Bible says the **effectual fervent prayer of a righteous man availeth much (*James 5:16*).**

God said you need to have a daily prayer. You should rejoice in hope, have patience in tribulations, and continue in prayer. Your prayer is the most powerful weapon that God is going to equip you with.
Your prayer life will bring you family back together! Your prayer life will open the windows of heaven and pour out a blessing that you wouldn't have room enough to see! Your prayer will keep you delivered. Your prayer will prevent temptation, Amen! Praise God! Your prayer will bring you to the victories of life.

I want to encourage you with this today. We are going to a higher mountain. We are going to a prayer mountain. We are going to graduate from this school of prayer and we are going to prevail! Look around!

There is trouble in every neighborhood, horrific things that people right now are going through. Someone may overdose tonight. Someone may die in a car crash tonight. Things happen daily!

However, if we stand united and pray, we can stop the tragedy from unfolding. We can reverse the curses. No matter what is taking place in your city, we can come together in our communities and go from Sin and Shame to GLORY!!!

Chapter Three
The Glory after the Deliverance of Addiction
Ultimate Judgment

The Shame of Addiction

Before we talk about the shame of addiction, I would like to talk about ultimate judgement.

And as it is appointed unto men once to die, but after this the judgment.
Hebrews 9:27

Driving out of Control

One horrible night, during the final stages of my addiction prior to my conversion to Christ, I was driving on the north side of Gulfport, Mississippi shortly after getting high with a co-worker. We went to score more dope and had two drug dealers riding in the back of my BMW, way past midnight. My life as I knew it was about to end...in sin. I felt death in my car. It was as if my life was on a movie screen and I was writing the last script.

As I was driving, I could see the drug dealers in my rearview mirror and hear with my own ears that they were contemplating a murder. All of a sudden, in the midst of my sin, I began to scream in a rage.
It confused the conspiracy of my death and immediately the drug dealers exclaimed, "Stop the car!", and they jumped right out.

I assumed they thought I had lost my mind. This was such a close call and almost the last call of my life. The Lord has since shown me that even in the midst of my sin, He was raining down Grace upon me.

That ye may be the children of your Father which is in heaven: for he maketh his sun to rise on the evil and on the good, and sendeth rain on the just and on the unjust.
Matthew 5:45

I give God all the glory. I believe it was my mother's prayers that stop the death angels that night.

I was in so much bondage in the midst of my sin. It was shameful in the beginning to talk about it, but now I am trying to help as many as I can with my story.

The School of Shame

Were they ashamed because of the abomination they have done? They were not even ashamed at all; they did not even know how to blush.
Just like the false prophets and wicked priests; who when they committed idolatry, or any other sin, and led the people into the same by their doctrine and example, yet, when reproved for it, were not ashamed, being given up to a judicial hardness of heart, they had neither shame nor fear.
Jeremiah 6:15

Shame, guilt, and condemnation are similar in that they all have to do with sin, but different in degree, duration, and scope.

Shame is an intense feeling of dread, anxiety, or anguish that makes you wish you could evaporate; extreme humiliation and remorse; a despairing of life from abject embarrassment.

Guilt is realizing you have done wrong, usually for some particular sin.

Condemnation is being sentenced (convicted) for doing wrong.

Shame is deeper than guilt. It is not based on having done something wrong so much as a soul ache of being wrong at the core.
Shame is more piercing than condemnation where the reality of judgment is mentally or
spiritually apprehended from an outside arbitrator, such as satan and his demonic spirits.
A person chosen to decide a dispute or settle differences, especially one formally empowered to examine the facts and decide the issue in one life, is trying to cover-up, or should I say, hiding the sin.

With shame we palpably feel our own depravity in vivid self-realization.

With this definition, what could possibly be the benefit of shame in the lives of the believers?

_____
_____
_____
_____
_____
_____
_____
_____

Where did all the shame come from? What can we learn from the shame from our past? How does God use shame in our recovery?

_____
_____
_____
_____
_____
_____

The Case For Shame - Teaching points

Wake from this drunken fit; live righteous lives, and cease to sin; for some have no knowledge of God: I speak thus in order to move you to shame.
1 Corinthians 15:34

Paul rebuked the Corinthians for evidently entertaining the thought that there is no future resurrection of the church.

> *I say this to put you to shame.*
> *1 Corinthians 6:5*

Thus, he checks their puffed-up spirit.

> *That you may remember and be ashamed.*
> *Ezezial 16:63*

> *O God, You know my foolishness; and my sins are not hidden from You. Because for Your sake I have borne reproach; shame has covered my face.*
> *Psalm 69:5,7*

> *For he himself endured a cross and thought nothing of its shame [NIV: scorning its shame] because of the joy he knew would follow his suffering.*
> *Hebrews 12:2*

The Case Against Shame - Teaching points

> *"Do not fear, for you will not be ashamed; Neither be disgraced, for you will not be put to shame; for you will forget the shame of your youth."*
> *Isaiah 54:4*

Then you will know that I am in Israel, that I am the Lord your God, and that there is no other; never again will my people be shamed.
Joel 2:27

For it is contained in Scripture, "See, I am placing on Mount Zion a Cornerstone, chosen, and held in honour, and he whose faith rests on Him shall never have reason to feel ashamed."
1 Peter 2:6

Is shame good or bad? Useful or destructive?

_____
_____
_____
_____
_____
_____
_____
_____

Therefore the showers have been withheld, and no spring rains have fallen. Yet you have the brazen look of a prostitute; you refuse to blush with shame.
Jeremiah 3:3

"Were they ashamed because of the abomination they have done?"
Jeremiah 6:15

When Simon Peter saw this, he fell down at the knees of Jesus, and exclaimed, "Master, leave my boat, for I am a sinful man."
Luke 5:8

What is your response to this scripture?

_____
_____
_____
_____
_____
_____
_____
_____

The Problem of Self Confidence And Pride

"Oh, Simon, Simon, do you know that Satan has asked to have you all to sift like wheat?--but I have prayed for you that you may not lose your faith. Yes, when you have turned back to me, you must strengthen these brothers of yours." Peter said to him, "Lord, I am ready to go to prison, or even to die with you!" "I tell you, Peter," returned Jesus, "before the cock crows today you will deny three times that you know me!"
Luke 22:31-34

Peter was a boaster, being confident in himself. Like us, he was prone to make promises to God and then to blow it in actual experience, leading to the condemnation of shame.

satan is attacking your faith and demanded to take you apart. We need to recognize the power of satan. satan is real and his power is great.

Do you feel that satan is trying to take your faith and leave it in pieces? Do you recognize that satan wants to sift and ruin you?

_____

_____

_____

_____

_____

_____

_____

You are under attack if you are trying to profess faith in Jesus and give your life in passionate pursuit of him! The apostle Paul says that the evil one is shooting flaming arrows at you (*Ephesians 6:16*)!

Jesus, Our Intercessor

Jesus says that he has prayed on behalf of Peter. Jesus is making intercession.

What does this mean for Peter?

_____

_____

_____

_____

_____

_____

_____

_____

Read and listen to the rest of verse 32. Peter can turn again and strengthen the brothers.

This word "turn" that Jesus uses is the same word found in *Acts 3:19* when Peter preached to Jerusalem, ***"Repent therefore, and turn back, that your sins may be blotted out."***

The word "turn" is speaking about repentance.

> *Brethren, if any of you do err from the truth, and one convert him;*
> *²⁰ Let him know, that he which converteth the sinner from the error of his way shall save a soul from death, and shall hide a multitude of sins.*
> *James 5:19-20*

For they themselves shew of us what manner of entering in we had unto you, and how ye turned to God from idols to serve the living and true God.
1 Thessalonians 1:9

For ye were as sheep going astray; but are now returned unto the Shepherd and Bishop of your souls.
1 Peter 2:25

James used this word, "turn", to speak of one who wanders from the truth but is brought back. (*James 5:19-20*)

I am convinced this man was with him."
"Man," replied Peter, "I do not know what you are talking about." And immediately, while he was still speaking, the cock crew. The Lord turned his head and looked straight at Peter, and into his mind flashed the words that the Lord had said to him... "You will disown me..." ...and he [Peter] went outside and wept bitterly.
Luke 22:59-62

We all had some times in our life denied Jesus by our actions.

The Saviour had been standing in the upper part of the room, which was probably roofed over, while Peter and the rest were down below in the courtyard, which was open to the sky, and therefore they needed a fire to warm them. Jesus had been standing before his judge; but on a sudden, as the cock crew, he "turned, and looked upon Peter."

Like Peter, we have been declared guilty!

God's Method for Turning Us Into True Servants

...so that you may bear your disgrace and be ashamed of all you have done... You will bear the consequences of your lewdness and your detestable practices.
Ezekial 16:54,58-61

This was the turning point for me into those who have surrendered to Jesus Christ.

These shameful failings are indeed painful, but the word of God can save a sin-sick soul.

For after I turned back, I repented; and after I was instructed, I smote on my thigh; I was ashamed, and also humiliated, because I bore the reproach of my youth.
Jeremiah 31:19

REPENTANCE RESULTS IN:
1. Conversion
2. Sins blotted out
3. Refreshing

Repent ye therefore, and be converted, that your sins may be blotted out, when the times of refreshing shall come from the presence of the Lord.
Acts 3:19

Repentance is the best way to deal with our past. Every time we get into the Bible, we receive instruction. Every time we hear a word from God, whether by preaching or by teaching, God is trying to give us wisdom in our situations. God never intended for your situation to have you. God has created you with dominion to control your situation.

Oh, the depth of the riches of the wisdom and knowledge of God! How unsearchable his judgments, and his paths beyond tracing out! "Who has known the mind of the Lord?" or "Who has been his counselor?" "Who has ever given to God, that God should repay him?" For from him and through him and to him are all things. To him be the glory forever! Amen.
Romans 11:33-36 (NIV)

What "made" Paul so happy? How can the shame of the fact that all of us have been dangerously, critically disobedient end up as being to God's praise and glory?

_____

_____

_____

_____

_____

_____

_____

_____

Answer:
The Contrast of Pharisee and the Really Transformed Servant

It doesn't matter what you have done, your success is in your surrender. If you want to come out, God's grace will bring you from sin and shame you shall be delivered by his glory.

Anointing His Feet

One of the the Pharisees asked him over for a meal. He went to the Pharisee's house and sat down at the dinner table. Just then a woman of the village, the town harlot, having learned that Jesus was a guest in the home of the Pharisee, came with a bottle of very expensive perfume and stood at his feet, weeping, raining tears on his feet.
Letting down her hair, she dried his feet, kissed them, and anointed them with the perfume.

When the Pharisee who had invited him saw this, he said to himself, "If this man was the prophet I thought he was, he would have known what kind of woman this is who is falling all over him."

40 Jesus said to him, "Simon, I have something to tell you."

"Oh? Tell me."

41-42 "Two men were in debt to a banker. One owed five hundred silver pieces, the other fifty. Neither of them could pay up, and so the banker canceled both debts. Which of the two would be more grateful?"

43-47 Simon answered, "I suppose the one who was forgiven the most."

"That's right," said Jesus. Then turning to the woman, but speaking to Simon, he said, "Do you see this woman? I came to your home; you provided no water for my feet, but she rained tears on my feet and dried them with her hair. You gave me no greeting, but from the time I arrived she hasn't quit kissing my feet. You provided nothing for freshening up, but she has soothed my feet with perfume. Impressive, isn't it?

She was forgiven many, many sins, and so she is very, very grateful.

48 Then he spoke to her: "I forgive your sins."

*49 That set the dinner guests talking behind his
back: "Who does he think he is, forgiving sins!"*

*50 He ignored them and said to the woman, "Your
faith has saved you. Go in peace."
Luke 7:36-50*

Saving faith for my next book, "Oh how I love Jesus,
because He first loved me!"

*For God has bound all men over to disobedience so
that he may have mercy on them all. Oh, the depth of
the riches of the wisdom and knowledge of God!
Romans 11:32-33*

*"That is why I tell you that her sins, many as they
were, are forgiven; for she has so much love. But the
man who has little to be forgiven has only a little
love to give."
Luke 7:47*

Love demonstrated by forgiveness

For we know from what bondage He saved us, and we
feel the shame as evidence as the glory of his divine
deliverance; therefore, we cannot help but praise
Jesus for saving us from the gutter!

I waited patiently for the Lord; he turned to me and heard my cry. He lifted me out of the slimy pit, out of the mud and mire; he set my feet on a rock and gave me a firm place to stand. He put a new song in my mouth, a hymn of praise to our God. Many will see it and fear and put their trust in the Lord.
Psalm 40:1-3

Many, O Lord my God, are Your wonderful works which You have done; And Your thoughts toward us cannot be recounted to You in order; If I would declare and speak of them, They are more than can be numbered.
Psalm 40:5

The Residue of Shame and the Eternity of Love

Our attempts at love before were short lived and inconsistent.

What a wretched man I am!
Romans 7:24

Shame is the "school of love" in Christ. Have we dropped out before graduating?
Your pressure brings power. Can you hold up and pressure?
Can we still hold your head up in the mist of your trial?

_____

_____

_____

_____

_____

_____

_____

_____

If we say that we have no sin, we are deceiving ourselves, and the truth is not in us. If we confess our sins, He is faithful and righteous to forgive us our sins and to cleanse us from all unrighteousness. If we say that we have not sinned, we make Him a liar, and His word is not in us.
1 John 1:8-10

Returning to our first Love

Then shall they deliver you up to be afflicted, and shall kill you: and ye shall be hated of all nations for my name's sake. And then shall many be offended, and shall betray one another, and shall hate one another. And many false prophets shall rise, and shall deceive many. And because iniquity shall abound, the love of many shall wax cold.
Matthew 24:9-12

I know thy works, and thy labour, and thy patience, and how thou canst not bear them which are evil: and thou hast tried them which say they are apostles, and are not, and hast found them liars: And hast borne, and hast patience, and for my name's sake hast laboured, and hast not fainted. Nevertheless I have somewhat against thee, because thou hast left thy first love. Remember therefore from whence thou art fallen, and repent, and do the first works; or else I will come unto thee quickly, and will remove thy candlestick out of his place, except thou repent.
Revelation 2:2-5

Jesus Christ

Looking unto Jesus the author and finisher of our faith; who for the joy that was set before him endured the cross, despising the shame, and is set down at the right hand of the throne of God.
Hebrews 12:2

Let your attitude to life be that of Christ Jesus himself... He humbled himself by living a life of utter obedience, to the point of death, and the death he died was the death of a common criminal. That is why God has now lifted him to the heights, and given him the name above all names.
Philippians 2:5,8-9

Shame Turns into Humility

Shame - the painful feeling arising from the consciousness of something dishonorable, improper, ridiculous, etc., done by oneself or another.

I was overcome with shame. Shame produces humility and humility opens us up to the spirit of God which brings about deliverance from brokenness. It causes me to lift my head up.

> *...looking to Jesus, the founder and perfecter of our faith, who for the joy that was set before him endured the cross, despising the shame, and is seated at the right hand of the throne of God.*
> *Hebrews 11:2*

God has revealed the glory of the way in which He is saving us.

> *But God, who is rich in mercy, for his great love wherewith he loved us, Even when we were dead in sins, hath quickened us together with Christ, by grace ye are saved.*
> *Ephesians 2:4-5*

> *"Now I, Nebuchadnezzar, [after the shameful rebuke of the Lord] praise and exalt and glorify the King of heaven, because everything he does is right and all his ways are just. And those who walk in pride he is able to humble."*
> *Dan 4:37*

The song of Moses [a debilitating prophetic song of the failings of Israel] the servant of God and the song of the Lamb: "Great and marvelous are your deeds, Lord God Almighty. Just and true are your ways, King of the ages."
Revelation 15:3

So they went, rejoicing that they had been considered worthy to suffer shame for His name.
Acts 5:41

It's Time to Gather and Seek The Lord.

Gather together, gather together, O shameful nation, before the appointed time arrives and that day sweeps on like chaff, before the fierce anger of the Lord comes upon you, before the day of the Lord's wrath comes upon you. Seek the Lord, all you humble of the land, you who do what he commands. Seek righteousness, seek humility; perhaps you will be sheltered on the day of the Lord's anger.
Zephaniah 2:1-3

"Then I [the Lord] will go back to my place until they admit their guilt. And they will seek my face; in their misery they will earnestly seek me."..."Come, let us return to the Lord. He has torn us to pieces but he will heal us; he has injured us but he will bind up our wounds. After two days he will revive us; on the third day he will restore us, that we may live in his presence."
Hosea 5:15-6:2

From the gutter, we must be filled with the Holy
Spirit to transition into ministry.

By faith the people passed through the Red Sea as on
dry land; but when the Egyptians tried to do so, they
were drowned.
Hebrew 11:29

"But I have prayed for you, Simon, that your faith
may not fail. And when you have turned back,
strengthen your brothers."
Luke 22:32

Preaching Nuggets for the Exhortation

With the power of prayer comes the power to bind. We have power to loose. We have power to take authority over unseen danger. We have the power to be great men and women of God. There is nothing too hard for God! Men need only to get on their knees and cry and begin to seek God, Amen! Seek the face of God instead of the hand of God. A lot of times we are looking for handouts. We need to come before God and begin to worship Him. We need to come before God and just adore Him.

Our father, which art in heaven, hallowed be thy name, thy kingdom come, thy will be done.

His will is His word, Beloved. If we pray God's word, Amen, we will get results! We have to study. You don't have to read the bible all night long to get a revelation. Just read something that is going to soak in your spirt and pray that Word from God. There was a time that Jesus was going up into Gethsemane, and he told his disciples to watch and pray unless they enter into temptation. They were so tired, they were succumbed to troubles and they fell asleep. Jesus told them to sleep on. Praise God! He was just showing us that men sometimes become bewildered. We got slothful, overtaken by the devices of our adversary.

I've come to tell you that God is going to bring you to a higher level in your prayer life. That is the most important gift God has given me and I do know that the power of God prevails through my prayer. It's not my title that makes me. Praise God, it's not who people say I am, it is who God says I am, Amen! By communicating with God, I feel better about myself. If I don't get a hand clap, if I don't get an Amen, I know I can get in touch with Jesus. He is never busy; He is always there.

If you call on him he will come near. I believe in that. I believe the same God that did it for me can do it for you. I believe if you are persistent in the things of God, He is going to bring you to a higher level in your life. He is going to bless your family. He is going to pour out blessings that you will not have room enough to receive. This is your season this is your time, Beloved! If you believe that, I want you to come in agreement with me in the power of prayer. I want you to know that this is the time for us to turn our hearts towards God. As you read this meditation and devotion on the school of prayer, I want you to discover a habitual prayer life! AMEN!

Chapter Four
Ministry in the Glory
Fact of Redemption

The Glory of God and the Fact of Redemption

Forasmuch as ye know that ye were not redeemed with corruptible things, as silver and gold, from your vain conversation received by tradition from your fathers.
1Peter 1:18

Deliverance is the power of Jesus showing up in man's life. There is no way to break that cycle of sin through individual human effort.

So many say, "I could quit any time I really wanted to". But when you get delivered you won't start back up again unless you enter back into sin. Quitting is what one does for himself. Deliverance is what God does for you.

The fact is that God can restore the family!

- The glory of healthy relationships
- The glory of knowing who we were created to be
- The glory of being used by God
- The glory of hope
- The glory of a blessed future
- The glory of eternal life after

Spending two decades dealing with my addiction was too much for me but it was nothing for Jesus Christ!

If the Son therefore shall make you free, ye shall be free indeed.
John 8:36

Everyone has a Story

Everyone has a story and only God can bring it to glory. There is the good, the bad, and the ugly in every creation, every culture, every race, in every community. Our nation as well as our country, our state, city, neighborhood, family; all have been affected by sin. All have sinned and come short of the glory of God. Now it's time for us to experience the full glory of our deliverance in Jesus Christ.

Whether you're "rich or poor" it doesn't matter. Only what you do for Christ will last. In the mid 80's I owned a 325i BMW convertible. As nice as this vehicle was, I couldn't fully enjoy it and appreciate it because of the lifestyle that I was living - the fast paced life - driving on a highway to hell. My life was not in the perfect will of God, and I did not have long to live.

There is a lesson for all of us to learn, that no matter how hard you work and how much money you make, it is all in vain unless you rid yourself of sin. Sin has a price and once it's been paid, you will not even be able to enjoy the fruit of life. Life will become meaningless, miserable, and sad. Troubles will lurk around. No matter what you do, how well you dress, how polished your life seems from the outside, how well you talk the "talk", there is no real joy to be had unless you confess. Just making mention of the car began to give me trouble in my soul. Even though the car looked immaculate when it was washed and clean, the motor was still messed up, just hidden from sight. No matter how good we look or how fast we may run, if we don't deal with what is on the inside, it will all fall apart and lead to pride.

Bible Verses About the Glory of God

Who being the brightness of [his] glory, and the express image of his person, and upholding all things by the word of his power, when he had by himself purged our sins, sat down on the right hand of the Majesty on high.
Hebrews 1:3

For of him, and through him, and to him, [are] all things: to whom [be] glory forever. Amen.
Romans 11:36

Jesus saith unto her, Said I not unto thee, that, if thou wouldest believe, thou shouldest see the glory of God?
John 11:40

For all have sinned, and come short of the glory of God.
Romans 3:23

And the sight of the glory of the LORD [was] like devouring fire on the top of the mount in the eyes of the children of Israel.
Exodus 24:17

Arise, shine; for thy light is come, and the glory of the LORD is risen upon thee.
Isaiah 60:1

And blessed [be] his glorious name for ever: and let the whole earth be filled [with] his glory; Amen, and Amen.
Psalms 72:19

I [am] the LORD: that [is] my name: and my glory will I not give to another, neither my praise to graven images.
Isaiah 42:8

For the earth shall be filled with the knowledge of the glory of the LORD, as the waters cover the sea.
Habakkuk 2:14

Having the glory of God: and her light [was] like unto a stone most precious, even like a jasper stone, clear as crystal.
Revelation 21:11

And [that] every tongue should confess that Jesus Christ [is] Lord, to the glory of God the Father.
Philippians 2:11

To whom God would make known what [is] the riches of the glory of this mystery among the Gentiles; which is Christ in you, the hope of glory.
Colossians 1:27

O LORD our Lord, how excellent [is] thy name in all the earth! Who hast set thy glory above the heavens.
Psalms 8:1

Then shall thy light break forth as the morning, and thine health shall spring forth speedily: and thy righteousness shall go before thee; the glory of the LORD shall be thy reward.
Isaiah 58:8

Presently, I'm spending time in the glory of God, pastoring at Trinity Outreach Ministries.

I am serving the Lord with all humility of mind, and with many tears, and temptations, which befell me by the lying in wait of the Jews: And how I kept back nothing that was profitable unto you, but have shewed you, and have taught you publicly, and from house to house, Testifying both to the Jews, and also to the Greeks, repentance toward God, and faith toward our Lord Jesus Christ. And now, behold, I go bound in the spirit unto Jerusalem, not knowing the things that shall befall me there: Save that the Holy Ghost witnesseth in every city, saying that bonds and afflictions abide me. But none of these things move me, neither count I my life dear unto myself, so that I might finish my course with joy, and the

ministry, which I have received of the Lord Jesus, to testify the gospel of the grace of God.
Acts 20:19-24.

I am thoroughly enjoying my wife and my family. I am believing that God will allow me to touch many souls for His Kingdom. I enjoy what I am doing. I love the word of God and His people. I really don't deserve to be in the position that I am. I truly give all the glory to God.

I just took a week vacation to Cozumel, Mexico and Progresso, Mexico. It was a life changing experience and I needed that time away to reflect. I had plenty of time to think so I decided to finish this book after many years of praying, contemplating, and writing. One of my emotionally refreshing moments is when I am in nature. Being around the clear blue water, listening to the waves crash on the beach as the palm trees blow lazily in the wind...these are refreshing times for me.

The Bible says:

The righteous shall flourish like the palm tree: he shall grow like a cedar in Lebanon. Those that be planted in the house of the LORD shall flourish in the courts of our God. They shall still bring forth fruit in old age; they shall be fat and flourishing.
Psalm 92:12-14

Preaching Nuggets for the Exhortation

The land is sick. It's sick because of sin. It's sick because of the condition of people's hearts. It's going to take a parade of people to move this society toward a new direction. If the fate of our land is left in the hands of a politician, we might not get to where we need to be. We have to make a choice and that choice is to dedicate ourselves to seeking God's spiritual course and resolves. We are going to have to put our hearts and our minds, our bodies and souls, toward the things of God. We must persevere and press on toward the goal.

I come now to encourage you, my brother and sister. You are probably not feeling strong right now. You may be reading this book and you want to discover a better way of doing things. Start with prayer! Start with seeking God first and if you seek Him, you will find Him. You call on him he will draw near. This is the time to draw near to God. This is the time for you to pursue happiness in the Word of God and to attend your local church, whether that be in Pontiac Michigan and the surrounding areas, New Orleans, Louisiana, Picayune, Mississippi, Hattiesburg, Mississippi...wherever you may be. Maybe you're in Africa or China but no matter your physical location, God has a spiritual word for you in this season if only you settle down and begin to let Him enter into your heart.

He said, "Behold! I stand at the door and knock and if any man would hear my voice I would come in and sup with him. (*Revelation 3:20*)

God wants to come into the door of our life, Amen! He wants to get into our ear gates and get into our hearts and He wants us to begin to call out and cry out to him for a new direction, for a new outlook in this date and time. I do believe that we can change our city! YOU can change your city but you first must change the man. If you change the man, you can change the family, you can touch the wife, you can touch the children, and then you can touch the neighborhood. The neighborhood has a church and great families have the ability and the power to impact that neighborhood church. They, as a whole, begin to reach out within the surrounding community and people come together as hands and feet of Jesus. I believe it starts with one soul...one soul at a time, one prayer at a time.

You must pace yourself. You don't start off running a marathon by sprinting. The Bible says, "The race is not given to the swift nor the strong but he who endures until the end." (*Ecclesiastes 9:11*)

We're going to have to build up our endurance one day at a time, one prayer at a time, and allow God to come in our hearts. We have the opportunity to cry out to God and tell Him everything about us. We know that we're strong enough. We know that we are nothing without God. He knows that we have problems and He knows that we come short. All God wants us to do is communicate with Him. You're hearing this from someone who was highly addicted to crack cocaine, to alcohol, a man subdued by pornography and lust, who lied to himself and others, who had the spirit of pride and all the works of the flesh that might manifest. I believe I operated and flowed in the majority of them but I thank God for His grace and I thank God for His mercy.

There is no condemnation for those who walk in the spirit and not the flesh because the law of the life of Christ Jesus has made us free from the law of sin and death. I am not ashamed of the Gospel. I'm not ashamed to cry out to God. I'm not ashamed to confess that I have the victory but I still know that I can do nothing by myself. I need God every day and every hour. I need God to direct my steps and order my steps through His Word. I need God to lead me and guide me.

The Bible tells us to Trust in the LORD with all thine heart; and lean not unto thine own understanding. In all thy ways acknowledge him, and he shall direct thy paths. (*Proverbs 3:5-6*)

He tells us that the steps of a good man are ordered by the LORD: and he delighteth in his way. (Psalm 37:23) We need God to order up our steps. He tells us, "Fret not thyself because of evildoers, neither be thou envious against the workers of iniquity. For they shall soon be cut down like the grass, and wither as the green herb. (Psalm 37:1-2)

In this season He wants us to be in agreement with Him. How can two walk together except they agree? (*Amos 3:3*)

We must agree with the Word of God. We're going to have to confess to the Word of God and we're going to have to believe in the Word of God. This is the season right now to draw near to God. This is the time to open up our mouth. I was once an introverted person, quiet, sitting back in the shadows of life.

Chapter Five
Forgiveness in the Glory
Fact of Reception

The Fact of Reception - Forgiveness of sin

Looking into my father's eyes in his final days, I felt his hurt and his pain. He did not share too much with me and he really didn't have to because the Holy Spirit bears witness with my Spirit and his Spirit.

I will conclude this chapter by a sharing with you my heart concerning my father. Even though he wasn't in my life, it was important that I deal with my resentment and bitterness toward him by allowing the word of God to touch my heart.

It wasn't that easy! But the Holy Spirit revealed to me that this was a major area that was hindering me in my process of being all I can be with God.
I must say that no child ever asks to come into this world! We did not have a choice in that and I am no better than anyone else. The only regret that I have in my life is I wish I could have realized my value a lot sooner in life, and that I would be further along in the things of God. But I had to go through what I went through to make me who I am today. Somethings could've been avoided on my behalf, but I don't look on those things with regret, only forgiveness.

I believe we look for excuses for our bad behavior when we been hurt in life. We isolate ourselves in our insecurities, we compromise with worldly lust, and we do not commit ourselves fully to the spirit of the Lord.

With that being said, I take full responsibility for my failures, my insecurities, and my roller coaster struggles in life.

Personal Responsibility = Freedom

I would like to dedicate this chapter to my father, a man who I am completely unfamiliar with. He was a man of few words. He didn't have to express his love toward me, for I knew. I believe he was an introvert as well. I also believe he wanted to tell me so much in his last days but didn't have the words to do so.

My father died August 7, 2014 from lung cancer. I would not be here had it not been for him. I don't blame him for anything he did not do and I forgive him for the same. I wish I had more time with him in those latter years to share just some of the glory that comes from a father and son relationship.

He suffered the last days of his life, but he never complained in the midst of the suffering. I asked him the question, "Dad, have you accepted Jesus Christ as your Lord and Savior?" His answer was, "In my own way." I do believe that he had some time to make peace with God.

I would like to share with you that he truly inspired me. In order to get to this point, I had to forgive him. *I* had to let it go. I was feeling a certain way for years and I did not understand any of it. Sure, I blamed him at one time, but it really doesn't matter anymore. What does matter is that we walk in the spirit of forgiveness always and we allow the Spirit of the Lord to help is in the areas that are deeply rooted with bitterness and resentment.

There are many ways that Christians can be affected by bitterness. Regret, jealousy, and envy can all lead to feelings of bitterness and to an unhappy life. When a person is bitter, their life doesn't feel worth living. Don't let that happen to you! Turn to God and try to heal your bitterness.

The Bible is here and was written to help us deal with these bitter feelings. There are many Bible verses about bitterness. If you are trying to move past an event or situation in your life that has left you feeling this way, be sure to read your Bible you will find in the Word that bitterness is most definitely a hindrance.

My soul is weary of my life; I will leave my complaint on myself; I will speak in the bitterness of my soul. Job 10:1

And another dies in the bitterness of his soul, and never eats with pleasure.
Job 21:25

Even to this day is my complaint bitter: my stroke is
heavier than my groaning.
Job 23:2

You, which have showed me great and sore troubles,
shall quicken me again, and shall bring me up again
from the depths of the earth.
Psalms 71:20

The heart knows his own bitterness; and a stranger
does not intermeddle with his joy.
Proverbs 41:10

Let all bitterness, and wrath, and anger, and
clamor, and evil speaking, be put away from you,
with all malice.
Ephesians 4:31

Looking diligently lest any man fail of the grace of
God; lest any root of bitterness springing up trouble
you, and thereby many be defiled.
Hebrews 12:15

But if you have bitter envying and strife in your
hearts, glory not, and lie not against the truth.
James 3:14

He that said he is in the light, and hates his brother,
is in darkness even until now.
1 John 2:9

The Word of God *will* help you although you might not think it at first. Believe in yourself and in God. Accept the fact that reading the Bible and praying can help you in your times of trouble. Praying to God and working past your problems can help heal the bitter feelings in your life.

I will not even give satan the glory to charge my life as a generational curse. I had the best mother that anyone could ask for! No one ever put a gun to my head and told me to use drugs. I was driven away by my own dealings with sin and I had not fully submitted to the Spirit of the Lord. I thank God for forgiveness!!

I would like to close this chapter and expound just a little by teaching on the glory of forgiveness. I pray that you will allow the Lord to heal you in every area of your life. It is also my prayer that it doesn't take you as long as it took me to repent of the sin that so easily entangles. Deal with that shame!! To God be the GLORY for what He has done!!

The following is the obituary I wrote upon my dad's death:

God Brought Us Close

It was love at a distance that God brought us close! It doesn't matter where or how long the years have been, God's love heals all sins. Love just recognized and knew that, Dad, you made it in.

My Dad, a man of few words, who expressed his love and concern for his family with smiles and hugs. God has forgiven; and that is all that matters. It is the commitment that you made after.

You tried, you reached out, you did your very best, now your suffering is over, go ahead and take your rest.

You took pride in yourself, you sported as you dressed, now sport your white robe and your heaven's best.

It's not goodbye, just I will see you later. Enjoy your afterlife with our Creator.

Rest in peace and with much love from your son and stepson, your grandchildren, great-grandchildren, your family and all the people you love.

You left a legacy and you did not complain. I saw it in your eyes how you endured the pain.

Your toughness, your commitment, your love in your voice will always be strength for us. See you later and whenever I get low, I'll just think about the father who God brought us close!

SALVATION

THE MOST IMPORTANT RELATIONSHIP FOR EVERY ONE OF US IS OUR RELATIONSHIP WITH JESUS CHRIST. CHOOSING TO BELIEVE THAT HE IS WHO HE CLAIMS TO BE—THE SON OF GOD AND THE ONLY WAY TO SALVATION—AND RECEIVING HIM BY FAITH AS YOUR LORD AND SAVIOR IS THE MOST IMPORTANT DECISION.

WE WANT LIFE. HE IS LIFE. WE NEED CLEANSING. HE IS A DELIVER.

Now that you heard my story you too can receive God's glory by praying the sinner's prayer.

SALVATION PRAYER

Dear God in heaven, I come to you in the name of Jesus. I acknowledge to You that I am a sinner, and I am sorry for my sins and the life that I have lived; I need your forgiveness.

I believe that your only begotten Son, Jesus Christ, shed His precious blood on the cross at Calvary and died for my sins, and I am now willing to turn from my sin.

You said in Your Holy Word, Romans 10:9 that if we confess the Lord our God and believe in our hearts that God raised Jesus from the dead, we shall be saved.

Right now I confess Jesus as the Lord of my soul. With my heart, I believe that God raised Jesus from the dead. This very moment I accept Jesus Christ as my own personal Savior and according to His Word, right now I am saved.

Thank you Jesus for your unlimited grace which has saved me from my sins. I thank you, Jesus that your grace never leads to license but rather it always leads to repentance. Therefore Lord Jesus transform my life so that I may bring glory and honor to you alone and not to myself.

Thank you Jesus for dying for me and giving me eternal life. AMEN.

Preaching Nuggets for the Exhortation

The Prayer School of Recovery

If you are like most new believers, you're probably wishing you had some kind of guide or mentor to help explain the technicalities, the beginning stages of Christianity. Actually, clarifying the beginning stage would be a privilege and will help you get connected to your power source. You probably feel that you've got more pressing and ultimate needs now that life is worth living with new healthy habits.

Now you too can be what God called you to be. There is nothing stopping you, not one thing, not one person. There is no hidden agendas. There is open communication between you and God. You are now discovering your purpose. You are now discovering the greater strength that lies within you. Beloved, this walk is a great walk. This life is a great life. We have a great future that is ahead of us if we only pray without ceasing!

Praise the Lord, learning how to pray is the most important tool in recovery. Getting closer with God is the answer in recovery. The Spirit of the Lord will teach us how to pray if we have a heart to pray. Often times, we don't seek God. As a result we go on with empty agendas. We don't have power when we pray because we don't practice prayer. We must pray in and out of season. It is very important as we deal with recovery and deliverance to develop a healthy prayer life.

The most important moment in getting closer with God is true deliverance. Seeking God daily is vital to a new believer. In doing so, you will gain strength. The Bible says we should go from strength to strength, from faith to faith, from glory to glory. Often times we get discouraged with the trials and tribulations of this day and time because we fail to pray and in doing so, we fail to seek the formula for prayer. We MUST pray. We must check in with God. We must develop a closer relationship with God in order to make it. We cannot make it on our own!

So often, we forget to pray and we stay weak in our faith. We have to build ourselves up in holy faith, staying in line with the Holy Spirit. I want to empower you in your prayer life so you can have victory in your daily walk. You may ask yourself the question, "Now What?"

I will encourage you to pray, develop a close relationship with God. Begin to seek Him daily. When you feel low, seek God. When you are rejoicing, seek God. Stay in touch with God.

A lot of times, we have a tendency to go off and leave God behind. When in recovery, the enemy becomes very clever and tricky. satan bombards our minds and thoughts. A lot of times, we live a life in condemnation because of the things we have done to ourselves and others. One of satan's devices is to keep us thinking about what we have done. He wants us to live our life in regret.

God wants us to walk in to confession. Confession is our way to true salvation. I do believe that if we develop a healthy prayer life, we can be as strong as any other Christian. I want you to be encouraged, because God is no respecter of person. You have to start somewhere, so start by discovering your spiritual strength in the power of prayer. This only comes from seeking God with all your heart. The Bible tells us to ask, seek, and knock and the door shall be opened up to us. God wants to open up the heavens to us!!

Seeking the Kingdom of God is very important, and it is very vital that we stay connected. Prayer will keep you connected. This is going to get you to the next level in your walk with Christ. It is going to tell you what to do when you are feeling low. It is going to encourage you to continue to seek the face of God, to study and to show yourself-approved unto God. **Study to show thyself approved unto God, a workman who needeth not to be ashamed, rightly dividing the word of truth.** (*2 Timothy 2:15*)

It is going to instruct you in righteousness. It is going to build you up to be a strong prayer warrior. This is what God is calling for. This is where the transformation takes place, when you discover your secret place. The Bible says that, **"He that dwelleth in the secret place of the most High shall abide under the shadow of the Almighty."** (*Psalm 91:1*) If you abide in God's presence and you seek the Spirit of the Lord for your answers, I would encourage you not to make hasty decisions. I encourage you to check with God first. I encourage you to be all that you can be. A lot of times we have battlefields going on in our minds, but God gives us the power of prayer to cast down imaginations and bring every thought to the obedience of Christ.

We have to discipline ourselves in prayer. It is just like a marathon runner. You have to build up your endurance to get to long distances. You first start off with one mile, then you take the next step, then sooner or later you are running five miles. The same goes in your Christian walk. You must be conditioned to persevere and to strive towards excellence. That is what we are doing. We are trying to build ourselves up by building up our endurance, building up our faith, building up our relationships, and building up our character to be strong men and strong women for the Kingdom of God.

We know what it is like to be in sin. We know what it is like to come short of the glory. We know what it is like to be addicted and afflicted in our mind and our spirit with low finances and low self-esteem. Now is the time to get to a season of rejoicing where we can enjoy life, enjoy our families, be productive citizens, maintain the things that God has given us, and represent the Kingdom of God. I am very optimistic that you, too, have a chance to be all that you can be. I had a lot of life failures. I had a lot of life disappointments, but I am in a season of capitalizing on all of my mistakes through the help and the power of prayer. If God be for us, who can be against us?

We must discover healthy habits. We must spend time with God daily. There should not be a day that goes by that we have not gotten on our knees or meditated on God's Word or sought God on behalf of our endeavors. We are not calling ourselves to be the best Christians, but we are going to give God our best. We are going to try, we are going to strive, we are going to seek God daily, we are going to empower ourselves with the wisdom of God, with his Word. We are going to do what is required of us to be all that we can be.

The disappointments, the failures of the past are water under the bridge. Now we can live life more abundantly. Now that you believe in Jesus Christ and have decided to acknowledge him as your Savior, you're probably wondering what's next. You undoubtedly want to get to know Jesus Christ better and discover what being a Christian means to you. You may even wonder what you got yourself into, what God has done for you, what God wants you to do, and how can you have a heart like God's heart.

You made the best decision in your life when you chose to become a follower of Jesus Christ. Keep the momentum by learning what's next now that you are a Christian. It was never emphasized to me the importance of prayer. I heard people praying loud prayers but they really didn't have substance to me because I didn't know how to pray. Just like the disciples, I asked the Lord to teach me how to pray. I'm not saying that I've perfected it yet but we have to practice it because practice makes perfect. A lot of times we ask for the wrong things and for the wrong reasons but in this season God is building us up. I want to encourage you as I close, you're well on your way to graduating and going to a deeper level in your school of prayer.

PRAYER WITH AN ATTITUDE

Now it is very vital that we understand how we view God. To grow and communicate with God requires appreciation for His awesomeness and His wonderful works. We need to have a heart of gratitude and appreciation for what He has done. He's going to lead us down the avenues and He's going to deepen our heart-felt communication with Him so that we will tap into His divine glory. Only God can fulfil your days, bless every hour, bring miracles and healing, restoration, and recovery to your life. Only God works in people's lives.

It is good to rejoice and stress your praise to God, as we see this. But, another work of God is neglected by us in his creation. The universe is marred. Sin will stop us every time, short of the glory of God. Sin separates us from God. Sin will cause our prayers from not being heard. Sin will keep us in guilt. Sin will keep us in shame. Sin will take us from the glory.

I remember at my early stages of seeking God, how important it was to go to church and to begin to fellowship and praise God. Prayer was a vital part of my spiritual walk and growth with God. At the beginning of getting into the presence of God, I began to seek him early and I began to decree and declare that I needed Him more than anything. So when you're attitude is right towards God, that means your heart will be open to the things of God. As a result, God will bless you every day. With that being said, it's very important that we continue to seek His presence. Once you seek the presence of God, it's going to be alright. So begin to petition, begin to cry out, and begin to call on Him daily.

When we confess in prayer, when we repent in prayer, we are then well on our way to victory. That is the most important thing that we have - to persevere and to continue to press our way into the spiritual realm. Have a divine experience with God. Seek God first - in the morning, in the afternoon, and nightly--throughout the day. You don't have to have a special place to pray. It's when you pray. It's not so much how you pray, or who will hear you pray. Go into your secret closet and command your morning, command your day. Know that you're a man and woman of God, and that you love his Word and love Him. You are a child of God. You deserve the best. So make your connection.

I will encourage you, in that you develop a heart and a spirit of prayer, and put on the whole armor of God, so that you may be able to stand against the whiles of the devil. Plug into the power source and go through the classroom. We will go through the victories. We will go through the rewards of a dynamic prayer life. Welcome to the School of Prayer. There is no more sin. There is no more shame. It's time to tap into the GLORY!

About the Author

Pastor Carl Flowers is the Founder and President of Trinity Outreach Ministries in Picayune, Mississippi. He is also the Founder of the Oasis Community Development Center in Picayune, Mississippi. Pastor Flowers is the instructor of the ARRM Restoration Recovery Ministry and Director of the Covenant Bible College and Seminary Satellite Campus, which is designed to educated and strengthen the body of Christ by identifying their purpose in helping those struggling with addiction.

Pastor Flowers is a speaker, spiritual father to many, and a mentor. He and his wife, Julie, and the two children born of their union reside in Picayune, Mississippi.

For speaking engagements on recovery, please contact **pastorcflow@aol.com**

Apostle Flowers

Special Thanks

Special thanks to Julie Keene for her God given expertise in editing and publishing this divinely inspired book. A very special thank you to the Trinity Outreach Ministries Team for their prayers and encouragement for we are better together.
Special thanks to Jacob's Well Recovery Center for Women and Damascus Road Recovery Center for Men for allowing my wife and I to spread the Good News in ministering to those in recovery from addictions.
Thank you to Rose and Tanya at Xpress Copy Center in Picayune, MS for their beautiful design of the cover of this book.
Special thank you to my grandmother Vivian McLaurin and to my family, friends, and prayer warriors.
And last, but certainly not least, a very special thanks to my beautiful wife of 30 years, Julie Flowers, who was there for me through all my struggles and never left my side. She never ceased praying for me and believing with an expectant heart for more of God's glory as I ministered to others in the hopes of reaching millions of families in need of divine restoration as we pursue the vision He has shown us together.